ROMANCE

The Only Life

SAINT JULIAN PRESS

POETRY

Books by KEVIN MCGRATH

Fame (1995)
Lioness (1998)
The Sanskrit Hero (2004)
Flyer (2005)
Comedia (2008)
Stri (2009)
Jaya (2011)
Supernature (2012)
Eroica, and *Heroic Krsna (2013)*
In the Kacch, and *Windward (2015)*
Arjuna Pandava, and *Eros (2016)*
Raja Yudhisthira (2017)
Bhisma Devavrata (2018)
Vyasa Redux (2019)
Song Of The Republic (2020)
On Friendship (2024)
Romance: The Only Life (2024)
And *Causality In Homeric Song*
(forthcoming, 2025)
DIONYSOS: Nature Without Instinct
(forthcoming, 2025)

Praise for ROMANCE - The Only Life

"Kevin McGrath's poetry surges with one of the rarest of forces: a vision. In McGrath's heart, the chaos of history is redeemed by a teleology, a motion toward fellowship, toward communion, toward love. The great man has left us, but his words live on, calling us to stand face to face and see the other world within this world, and to praise it."

—Joseph Fasano

"Beautifully candid, each poem in Romance offers such a masterful clarity of perspective, that one can't help but read and re-read each poem, in awe of how much life each line holds. Kevin McGrath's masterpiece is a tapestry of love, friendship, and the essence of our human existence, woven into a backdrop of the steady progression of time."

—Maryam Hiradfar

"Kevin McGrath was such a wonderful person, mentor and poet/philosopher. Blessed to have spent so much time with him in our poetry group at Harvard ~ blessed to be able continue that loving relationship with his poetry."

—Gary Geissler

"This is a journey of love, life's most essential metaphor, through "the ardent force of time," landscape and seascape, language and silence, the seasons of nature and of life. It is a powerful Gospel or Veda of love, and I will turn to its beautiful verses again and again."

—Diana Eck

ROMANCE

The Only Life

Kevin McGRATH

SAINT JULIAN PRESS
HOUSTON

Published by
SAINT JULIAN PRESS, Inc.
2053 Cortlandt, Suite 200
Houston, Texas 77008

www.saintjulianpress.com

ISBN-13: 978-1-955194-40-2
Library of Congress Control Number: 2024948742

Cover Image: *Aegean Sea* by Prosser Stirling
Author Photo: Courtesy of Akos Szilvasi.

~ To Guy Murdo & Maximilien Guy ~

Per tanti rivi s'empie d'allegrezza
La mente mia, che di sé fa letizia
Perché può sostener che non si spezza.

Paradiso XVI,19-21

CONTENTS

FOREWORD

THIS is a book about human chronicle and existence in its most original and metaphorical form or, that one singular narrative which we all attempt to apprehend in our way, to imitate and emulate in sequence. Here, the fundamental element of time is the annual year, presented by the movement of shadow in both motion and inclination across the curved planes of our terrestrial planet. This temporal medium of the year frames and conveys those occasions where we receive the visitations that both exceed and generate experience and the knowledge which ensues. Within that cycle the natural modes of birth, reproduction, and death become stylised and dramatised by rituals of affection and disaffection and by the metaphors that summon, activate, and record those events. It is this natural world which informs us with our ground of being and the emotions which are generated by those occasions or ceremonies. Those initiating metaphors were first supplied by terrain and climate, by topography and field, long ago as early hominids walked about the earth. Before words and their acoustic register existed, landscape and the marine first indicated whom we were, and in this there occurred the experience of apperception; for paradoxically we then ceased to exist for a moment as we received that conceptual impetus. Nowadays we receive these tropes as we gather to ourselves the patterns and formulation of language which create awareness and consciousness. In sum, landscape is a prelude to language as the latter then forecasts how it is that we so move in life in terms of affect, company, and the grief of removal, the three tropes of narrative. This conspicuous fabric not only of all time but also of both form and impulse makes us so human and potentially beyond place and moment: the sovereign account of life and all sequence which we attempt to replicate, approximate, and recapitulate in time.

ROMANCE

The Only Life

ONE

HOW the universe disdains us
For all our untruth
Even the adamant star of dawn
Acknowledges our futility

As birds flock and fish school
Our mortality is inferred
Neither decent nor improper we
Transmit no consequence in life

So the hours simply curve
Bending with delight
And shadows walk beside us
About these invisible days

Days are embroidered now
With lions and young leopards
Those slim transient figures
Of beauty and precision

They do not perceive us
Or even know the words we say
Yet their gentle kindness
Is the source of our speech

We are merely touched
By the dust from their feet
And exposed we are so able
To continue in our way

They only love the future
Which is where they harvest breath
Inspired by anticipation
They do not tread this world

Like the ambition of a bride
Or promise of a groom
Or swallows who come and go
Always they return and stand

Charged with their amity
No being ever goes apart
They are elusive as we mourn
What it is they cannot say

Compassionate they disclose
Their lightness of perfection
And hand in hand they surpass
Our suffering and endurance

The darkness of our years is tilting
And soon we shall step outside
Stand apart from this old world
Leave no impression on the earth

Yet thanks to kind fortune
We have escaped demise
Gifts from the sky have clothed
The election of our time here

We are imbued by life and days
As the sky reaches down and
With its fingertips supports us
As we struggle to apprehend

What to say now as it goes
As the future consumes the past
We who held so many gifts
Do not know what we accomplished

TWO

WHERE a disc was thrown
In pleasure at the sea
We found ourselves becoming
More and more transparent

Lakes now lose their ice
Rivers flood their margins
The ocean gathers warmth
Changing from grey to blue

An infant snowdrop rises up
Newborn of the vernal year
And the dashing witch-hazel
Floating on a cold wind

Next the agile cadmium
Forsythia in stiff hedges
And the queenly crocus
With her majestic daffodil -

Avenues of candid pear
Magnolia and pure dogwood
So the year might advance
Like a dancer on the river

Light-footed among the trees
Or a pink hand upraised
Each novel day is reformed
Promising us life again

Fragrance of the year now
An ideal of perfect love
Where no destiny remains
Wind is the only living force

So we gave our hearts away
Pretending to be solitary
No one could conceive
That tempering of kindness

In the presence of a friend
Whose virtue so displaced us
Whose beauty was profound
Within our futile hearts -

Both musical and visual – we
Were conveyed by affection
Beyond fields of experience
And their mineral duration

With eyes closed we saw at night
That subtle lucid form like rain
Allowing us to exceed despair
Without desire recreated

In love there is no innocence
We submit to the unknown
Then taken by a silent hand
We are admitted to new ways

So much of life runs away
As we try to grasp that river
Only the reticent remains
Of friendship or even grief

You who walked beside us
Once laughed and made demands
Claiming affection as a right
And warmth at night as ritual

Now as we stand apart
And terminus approaches
We might never be extinguished
For we kept to your kind

For the end of experience
Is a ripening of weightless fruit
As from leaf to grain the feral
Makes beautiful our share

Apple trees and almonds
Can whiten our spring days
With their visceral honesty
A goodness they present

Yet in the vineyard now
Entering this light season
A late snow might conceal
The genius of perfect truth

THREE

THERE is a ship of light
Circling us in its way
Whose hull masts and sails
Move forever without ruin

In spring leaves and vines appear
Upon the timbers and the spars
And on the decks small croci
Fall beneath the mariners' feet

Flags and a sound of bells
Adorn the vessel as it goes
Making her so beautiful
That even birds pause in flight

Gulls flying fish and stars
Circulate the dark of night
Squalls approach as if
They were consciousness itself

This ship of earthly love or
Vessel of all emptiness
Marks a thin brief wake upon
The turquoise and aquamarine

There is only one just voyage
That we imitate and emulate
Our footsteps create a course
Which vanishes and reappears

Some are fortunate in love
Others wear a cloth of grief
A few discover the friend who
Might transport them out of life

Surrounded by a void we are
Yet the ship holds its point
More than destiny the compass
Knows of perfect islands

Each day at sea this lucid gift
Like a pearl grows opaque
Suffering and death only reveal
A triumph of constant loss

So build yourself a single vessel
That will always take you on
When dawn and midnight fail
And love and truth join hands

FOUR

NOW as the year advances
Towards its spherical height
All our devotion settles
To a voyage of days

The fragile hands of spring
Reach out to catch the air
Small dark sharpened leaves
Open to the new warmth

Now the year is crowned
As all the trees admire
The beauty of tall skies
Where moon and planets pause

At this apex and focus
Of all possible desire
At last we are escorted
And might exceed death

Grey lakes repeat the sky
Rivers run toward the sea
As we simply cross the earth
Pursuing so many paths

Daffodils upon the shore
Boats upon the moving water -
Warmth dryness the luminous
Amplify a still twilight

This is the absolute song
Unity of earth's perfection
Journey of male and feminine
Creating and recreating

For there is only one story
Ritual of our existence
As we walk through sunlight
Until we become nil

Brave crocus and hyacinth
Are delivered to our eyes
As a young king steps ashore
In the vision of his heroes

Magnolia and dogwood
Like true queens in life
Bring to the new air all
Their brief dignity of kind

Geese and heron return
To our present sight
Currents of wind and stream
Support their lightness

So the old year falls
Its footsteps now revive
And we follow in that way
Without personal direction

In our eyes time changes
Yet in our hearts we endure
The bounds of affection
Affinity we all crave

As swallows come and go
So too the blood within
Our heart leads us
To gather the unseen

For the love of swallows is
Perpetual and changeless
They only reiterate and
Renew the same music

Their slight weightless bodies
Accomplish in the light
A young annunciation
Beyond anything we know

FIVE

AUTUMN came and went its way
Of blood and luminosity
Then winter compressed us
With cold unlimited darkness

Now maiden spring is lovely
Unaware of its clear beauty
Until summer moves and makes
Us strong in our nakedness

Time like a ring encircles
Marries us in its eyes
In a slow procession of days
Where barefoot we follow –

To the wedding chamber
Then to the garden where
Children make us aware
Of what we have become

We only fall in love once
In this life and then
We surrender knowing
The rest does not change

No matter where we walk
Or where it is we sleep
Once our lips are touched
There is nothing to be held

This is the joy of losing
All we cannot say -
Kindness we have received
Like water is transparent

There is one just masterpiece
Drawing us from life -
We are given imperfection
So that we do not fail

For there are two roads here
And that courage of election
To be alone without warmth
Creates our fidelity

Even the wren knows this
Or the journeying swallow
Yet at birth we do not know
The promise we received

Victory is for the singular
For those whose home
Exists only in their heart
Thoughtless and unspoken

Now at this final moment
Of triumph in the light
We travel far from the world
Unbound from every love

Many women make their way
Toward where their men
Disappeared and there
They now become true lovers

Palms trees in the human heart
Flourish and give their leaves
So the chosen might be crowned
Made free of running blood

SIX

AN immanent grief now makes
Us human and so fragile
Like a perfect blade always
Lingering scarcely in our sight

Lean shadow now inclines
Marking thin vernal air
At night we touch each other
For darkness is all we know

In suave and umber shadow
Beneath a lucid shining noon
There is boundless quietness
As we walk into the light

Entering on a new terrain
As if a wafer that inspires
Our breath and speech to gasp
With unspeakable exhilaration

This new blond spring radiance
Quietly keeps us captive
As all secrecy now hides
A rare inhuman tuning

A slim bright print of trees
Holds us in its arms
So we love sparingly
Giving more than we betray

There is only one day
On which this might occur
Fraction of a brief instant
When we are so reformed

Then from the sky descends
A hand touching deeply
Within our guilty bodies
Drawing us from sleep

As if within a clear vessel
Submerged in lucid blood
The hand reaches taking
All that we might love

Like a spear that splits apart
The vivid sky and tears
Open our living tissue
In life we are remade

Passion is now stripped
And in perfect outline
The beauty of a naked figure
Revives us with its eyes -

Beneath the gathering stars
Where silently and evasive
We are undisguised by
This unbearable desire

This is how a wedding song
Which all brides admire
Like a vessel of perfection
Comes bearing all we know

So lovers stand upon a shore
Swallows dart across a lake
As if time and experience
Withdrew from their vision -

Renewed as if by nothing
Made entirely true and
Perfected by the visible
And then lightly touched

Now we open worldly eyes
Receiving glamourous dawn
Fulfilling this one ritual
Sacrifice made by love

Like the flight of a flawless swan
Or a summoning of bells
We participate in time
Then continue out of life

We waken then we sleep
Between which we are joined
Without pain or affliction
And conducted on our way

SEVEN

THESE spring rites of passion
As each moment we are led
Sacrificed upon the light
Buried within our eyes

May - when young men
And women walk together
Knowing what they desire
Yet unable to say its name

Or a couple pleased
To have lightly shared
Love and its only medium -
Outline of a human form

As two men who both love
One woman are not the same
So day and night surround
Us with an equal ardour

I have never seen my love
Wear clothes for she -
As we reveal the universe
Is darkened by the night

To all lovers then
Let your time exceed
Every passing moment so
You are never without kind

Balanced by this destiny
Driven by impulsive force
Yet all we breathe vanishes
Every word we say is lost

Unless we struggle to perfect
An unspeakable affection
Intimate with an unseen
Unbreakable transparency

Formed of dust and shadow
Made to rest upon a stone
The only truth we apprehend
Is the amity of being with one

There we might perceive light
Holding life within its arms
And know how phenomenal
We are and free to love

Both double and distinct now
We all pursue one same ideal
That mystery where men
And women create happiness

So be infinite and enjoy
How life never ends
Exchanging gifts of hands
And vision never closing

Always be abounding
In the infinity you hold
With your fingertips fulfill
The fortune of this place

In the springing of this time
Where beauty is composed
In complete goodness may
Your sunlight find its joy

EIGHT

Now the universe expands
Its hands explore our nature
Testing misery and sorrow
Against love's aspiration

Just like the geese and swallows
Travelers of wind and heaven
We reveal the intimate
As a means to take flight

A doe and her fawn pause
In yellow and dark-blue shade
Incautious of the world and
Its sharp ways of life and death

There is ceremony in this
As dark water and sky reflect
The certainty of companionship
And fabric of love's conception –

The woods and low declivities
Courtship of youth and birds
All tell of one affinity
The nature of admiration

As if from death we are
Reformed with clear perception
The darkness of shadow broken
Into hyacinth and forsythia

A perfect body is revealed
Untouched and supersensible
Perpetually without terminus
This is the lasting marriage

The formal nuptial of all
As the overt is offered -
Crowds of new white blossom
Dogwood and magnolia

All the wheels of beauty
Run across the earth now
Circling and returning as
We go hand in hand

An obdurate sky is hovering
Uncertain as to motive
As human life halts and craves
One rare emblem of the future

For in spring and vernal life
There is no perceiving
As impulse and imperative
Make our blood aware

With summer there is radiance
Shining eyes that cause
The touch of admiration when
We give ourselves in love

Then autumn fetches ruin
Desiccation of the sense
A falling down of gesture
And increasing slowness

Winter brings perspective
The significance of death
Our grain of understanding
And beautiful admission

N I N E

ACROSS our bodies on the grass
Pear and apple blossom fall
Making quiet our nakedness
These new young hours we share

So the year is refreshed
Love is founded once again
Even though we do not touch
Vision in our eyes is joined -

Crowned with this wreath of light
Diadem given by the sun
Garland of living tissue
Adorning our fragility -

White birds in lemon trees
Blue swallows in dashing air
As sunlight bends and curves
About all we give each other

This elevation of clear fire
Despite the world's disordering
Moves our bodies out of time
As we are dressed in blossom

Regardless of what we do
Or say from this point now
Nothing can be subtracted nor
Removed from this equality

So a perfect child is born
Called promise and all beauty
To whom we offer up our lives
This shining of the universe

All the animals on earth
Trees and all life at sea
All bend their necks now
In admission of this moment

Unclothed and recreated we
In this fulfilment of the year -
Our nakedness is truth itself
Nothing could be more apparent

Nothing more could be said
As we fell away from kind
Tumbling through the years
Away from all we have received

Like a bird struck in flight
Has no words nor memory
And turns its head to recall
The brief project of its journey -

Now glorious and radiant this
Fame of being without flesh
Even blood cannot cover
This permanence of just seconds

TEN

THE lightness of these days
Their instrumental harmony
Lucidity of grey shadow
Whose clarity is unspeakable -

Great rings of time surround us
Now with an urgency of birds
Creatures of transparency
Whose voice once gave us speech

We know nothing here on earth
Except for our duration
And when we tire of loving
All that we observe is light

Midsummer on a lake
Striking the water perfectly
In the depth light pauses
As if unwilling to move

Heron and swallow glide
As if in perpetual flight
Motionless they slowly pass
Incise the fluctuating air

On the river and the fields
Young men and woman go
Beautiful yet untelling
What it is they want on earth

Their flawless human body
Where sacrifice is performed
Each day on a warm hearth
Of carmine and radical dawn

Where blood even in sleep
Is driven by kindness
Running with a currency
That forbids all decease

Just as deer in shadow
Or a fox among the grain
Are unnoticed as they perceive
Our lives of reckless haste –

Superhuman or supernal
Eyes that watch us when alone
Never close nor turn aside
As all they do is merely wait

This boundless coincidence
Of falcon dragonfly and dove
As all experience is renewed
By an instant of no duration

Charisma of what we cannot say
As viridian becomes chrome
Prediction is impossible now
Given so much intimacy

A naked man and woman stroll
The mirror of a wet sea shore
Lion and lioness attuned
By movement of another body

Hand in hand their amity
Formed perfectly in their eyes
The timeliness of how they go
Reflects the sky above them

Beneath the depthless air they
Step in and out of days
The only truth that continues
Is the goodness they never say

Few in life admit perfection
This complete silvery zenith
For only when our aim is true
May we live so fluently

ELEVEN

IF the present is simply a lineage
Where breath meets breath
Promiscuous and superfluous
In both fullness and expiration –

Sunlight rides above us now
Fields are scythed and laid
Just as our ideal life
Pauses in this fluent time

Midsummer upon a lake
Where deer swim to the isles
Where an empty future waits
For days to recommence

From this perfect zenith now
There are only boundless rings
Where beauty walks unseen
Except for those who are alone

Shadow sleeps within our eyes
As we walk beyond the city
Evening fires are being charged
Smoke lies upon the ground

In the undulance of courtship
Conception breath and extinction
The artifice of time combines
Tempering the superhuman

The sky dismisses us so lightly
Its few ideals remain
As the spiraling and amorous
In which we are mere shells

Although we have been crowned
We still possess no wealth
Our bare hands are empty
Yet music is our burden

For we have scarcely stepped
Upon this flat blue world
Its stones trees and mountains
The glassy vessel of its heaven

If beauty truth and love
Are three coins we hold
They can never be withdrawn
For their worth is unknown

In these days of midsummer
As a lovely world declines
Light falls away from us
Receding on all sides

There can be no death
If love is well-designed
Yet pity always calls us back
Making us only kind

Now that we embark
Leave the coast and set out
Upon one more voyage
We are free at last to be alone

Even lovers cannot succeed
In dominating nakedness
Indestructible as fire they
Are simply mere pedestrians

Until a rare human life appears
Whose solitude transports us
Away from every promise
An emptiness we apprehend

Shadow enters to our hearts
The lovers fall aside
Evening fires are rekindled
Warmth and smoke become alive

T W E L V E

WALKING a thin dusty path
Along the old coast where grass
Was brittle and yellow with heat
We arrived at a rocky cove

There we undressed and swam
Diving into the ultramarine
The bay apart from the world
And you and I at last alone

Sinking into the coldness
Beneath the waves and light
We entered into a vision of life
The silence of a shipwreck

Long ago the vessel foundered
There was nothing now but ruin
As the sea above refracted
The day into this aquamarine

We swam for hours the decks
Where no mariner now walked
Looked into the cabins below
Where no passenger slept

No sails nor lines nor command
Ever moved about the ship
In the cool grey atmosphere
An aqueous world was unmoving

Without one sign of kind
Not even fish or weed or shell
Only sand and rust and decay
Were visible yet motionless -

A dark bell on the mast
Vanity written on its metal
Immobility – rotting quietness
Its only cry to the world

For days we swam that water
With its odour of salt and pine
Sleeping on the shore never
Wanting to abandon stillness

Then you were most perfect
So beautiful and justly true
Fragrance of your complete kisses
Bronze smoothness of your limbs

Beside you on the changeless beach
Night warm as immutable blood
As mercury sea covered our feet
Indestructible starlight touched us

The harmony of your flawless bones
Sweetness of your mouth
Warmth of your gladness during
This nuptial of a weightless world

We would never waken from that
Regardless of what years accomplished
Wherever we walked or rested
Those hours were the most enduring

Without thirst or hunger
Captive in the depth of bay
Timeless in a profound world
Where naked we submerged

THIRTEEN

WHEN we were newly young
We only knew the sunlight
Rain came once a year
We were welcomed by the sea

Sails went upon those waters
About dry stony islands
Fields were ploughed and grain
Threshed in changeless circles

Rivers never failed us
Their current was like love
Beneficent and permanent
Without source or terminus

Groves of trees and orchards
Offered their shining fruit
Marriages and betrothals
Brought happiness to thresholds

Now we listen to the rain
Wind as it tears the trees
Sound of cold waves breaking
Of darkness being driven

Yet all that goodness stays
Far inside our timeless heart
Those bare hills are in our eyes
We know all the narrow paths

So let us join hands again
Refind those weightless hours
Those warm unclothed days
When no one observed us

Once passion is received
It never changes only
Remains with us continually
As a promise we convey

In those days we kept
One justly intimate truth
Indelible and perfect
Inscribed by simple affection

Not even grief can touch
Those patterns that we found
Upon our bodies in the night
When sleep was so exceeded

FOURTEEN

RIVER – waves - a boat
Lake of human affection
Regardless of suffering there
Is always a present romance

Where a shining hidden tree
Grows far within the blood
Whose blossom and whose fruit
Lightly sustain our ideals

For water – we improvise
Pretending that we drink
From pools of happiness or
Cisterns where we believe

There remains an undertow
Beneath the waves drawing
Us out onto an open sea
Where love becomes a vessel

Ship where we might advance
Into a transient light
And a round table where
We dine upon earthly ordeals

So many mutable wheels
Balance us in their turn
As smooth as a bird we go
Throughout time unnoticing

The queen of the year now walks
Touching us with her hands
Offering us a gift of grain
Water that none might resist

In the singular eyes of a woman
There is an open universe
In men a solitary moment
Yet they both love equally

Love is our only knowing
We dress ourselves each day
Chastening our eyes and
Ordering our affection -

Like two women adored
By one man - or two men
Pursued by a single woman
Where each find tranquillity

Time travels through human life
With roots branches and leaves
Changing and achieving till
One day there is no tree

Rainfall darkness wind
These now fill our sleeping lives
With benefit and moral truth
Until we are at last aware

From clouds and rain to streams
We fluctuate on a current
Idle waves where we might love
Secure from all indifference

So the romance of this world
Is like a net where caught
We are caressed for a while
Then returned to darkness

FIFTEEN

FULL moon and dog days
Sleepless nights - humid dawns
Dragonflies upon a lake
Swallows above the river

A voice from the sea is calling
As we swim out onto the water
Through low viridian morning
Languid herons break the air

Like human awareness falling
An osprey patrols the sky
Diving upon the black waves
In search of its own life

As Sirius rises out of darkness
Dominating with its fire
Intangible is this flame
That does not touch the body

Miraculous ephemeral days
We do not see their light
Nor the forceful ingenuity
Of creatures passing unnoticed -

Lioness panther hawk
Crossing now before the sun
Pouring out a scarlet liquid
In which all life disappears

Julian days when the year
Hovers above the earth
Directing warmth and lightness
As grain and grass are reaped

The sun is no more pursuing
And the red lion's blood
No more colours the bed
In circles about the lovers

Their humanity is threshed
And their small wealth placed
On altars made of stone and
Their accomplishment weighed

All couples possess those few
Rare and perfect minutes
Where kindness is esteemed
So the world might survive

Yet few give themselves in love
Or complete their admission
So a voice from the sea calls
Them home for unachievement

Most of life is lost - mislaid
Never to be reclaimed
Except for a few instants
When naked truth makes its way

SIXTEEN

EARLY Sunday morning
Without traffic or human sound
Even trees are unmoving
There are no voices anywhere

Then sometimes when we sleep
We turn to bronze or stone
Scarcely breathing – fixed
Motionless as complete time

We might become a river
Easy with currency and flow
Where birds fish and small
Quadrupeds live in company

Sometimes we walk a dry terrain
Where hawks and foxes live apart
Where heroes wandered footloose
Once - where songs were made

What should one then say
To shadows or open windows
Those places where immortals
Stand and quietly observe

As in this predawn time
When a lion sun bites
Its paws and blood runs out
Upon a barely sleeping world -

This silence is a vehicle
Medium in which we depart
As if upon a boundless voyage
Aboard a ship without mariners

A vessel that is both wild
And savage yet benign
At rest and compassionate
Where water runs toward water

There is no end to time
For those who close their eyes
Without intention or volition
In that light universe

You are always present
Quiet or perhaps strong
Clear vitality in me moving
With all the patience of the world

Then sometimes I waken slowly
Longing to remain in night
Where you and I might range
The perpetual land we love

So I wander candid days
Admiring you so inwardly
Yet we might not ever meet
Until oblivion comes again

The sound of leaves is changing
As is the darkness of shadow
Wind circulates its source
As sunlight presently declines -

Sunday morning when we go
Where neither life nor death
Takes our arm and says -
There is nothing but election

S E V E N T E E N

THE shadow on the dial
Shows no more southern days
As the edges of our life
Become a world unseen

Birds go and then the leaves
Small quadrupeds vanish
Where there is no vision
There is only dissolution

Life's golden wave was moving
Through the grass and blurred
As time became opaque and we
Walked across our emptiness

Then you touched me everywhere
Like summer you were light
Without thorns or any wound
You flourished beside me

That diamond aperture
Where we were captivated
By so many intransitive lives
Who observed our passion

How was it that we loved
When those shadows touched
Covering all the kindness we
Held as long as possible

Night was in your blood then
Your body was like day
I traced all your beauty as
My hands outlined your shape

Your voice was like a vessel
In which the world sailed
I thank you for that solitude
Which kept us so close

How we swam that summer
Lakes rivers and offshore
Love was unique and just
As we slept beside ourselves

The movement on the dial now
Sinks into the grey slate
Although we do not see it
We follow where it goes

EIGHTEEN

THREE swans circle passing
About the perfect light
We cannot hold their beauty
Nor run from its pursuit

Like the skull of an eagle
With its vast empty orbits
Or the body of a falcon
Decaying on a lake shore -

There is no refuge despite
This brevity of experience
How it is we only repeat
All that we ever received

The perpetual swan of life
Both animal and formal
Whose anticipation of the future
Is soundless – unavoidable

In this marriage of only life
There are no wedding guests
Nuptial rites occur at dawn
The invisible lover is embraced

All of kind now vanishes
Except for that one proposal
For where a heart existed
A bare universe now streams

Even death becomes transitory
We move toward another station
Where nothing is recalled and
There are no signs of ambition

As a dancer before a loom
Who discards all clothing
Whose nakedness is perfect
As light plays in marriage –

To that sanctuary we now go
And in that changeless air
The beautiful becomes explicit
And the true has no weight

At times that is unbearable
And yet it is our only truth
That bareness of the universe
Which lightly holds us in its arms

NINETEEN

THERE are archers in the light
Who propose to us now
Whose songs say – come away
For we need you in our arms

A million years of emptiness
Cannot assuage your appeal
To apprehend here on earth
The fame of human worth

All the fast runners know
How to surpass time
Just as lovers are aware
Of what no one else can say

In fabulous unforced midnight
When humanity is dyed
Where the dance is composed
And masks are appointed -

We are found unsure
In the exhaustion of suffering
Torn apart by formlessness
That drives our enduring

So may your years be round
Opening and enclosing
Transporting you in darkness
As if you were a bride

May these arrows bring you
Beyond worldly life
For your beauty is complete
You cannot be diminished now

The aim of every sunrise
Whose passion is to love
Exposes well the 19universe
With this musical design

If the bow is right friendship
Then what it achieves
Is more than affection
And perfection of our kind

These missiles make us true
As they pass between the eyes
Of men and women as they meet
In the evening of desire

TWENTY

In the end it is only chance
The ephemeral and random
That exposes life for us
The last face we recall -

It is not the plan nor
Ambition like a magnet
But the sudden unexpected
Stroke of a hand or eye

The walk of lovers is perpetual
Just as the approach of night
Both curve as they advance
Changeless with perfect vanity

The virtue of a lioness
Or of a shell or any star
Cannot be collected or
Reserved from earthly transit

If patience is the only way
We may not compete with time
Romance or sacrifice – which
Is it that reveals the most

Although we do not know it
At the bottom of the stair
Destiny stands and waits
With new cloth prepared

Then in profound solitude
We lie upon thin dry grass
Our head upon a stone
As we wander with the clouds

We were not born for daily life
But for the love of genius
This was told when we were young
Yet few perceived those footsteps

For only in retrospect does light
Reveal itself to human eyes
So that was it – they say
As they experience the transport

From the trees no leaf falls
Neither satiation nor remorse
This truth is soundless - casual
Composing all our vision

TWENTY ONE

Now we surrender our days
Worn impervious being at sea
Bending over a smooth oar
Drawing down an evening sail

Our years were like a king
Who walked about the level earth
Visiting walled harbours
Overruling with each pace

No one knows where we are
Nor recollects our name
There is no body to recall -
Making sleep a little easier

This is our truthful freedom
Although there is scarce bread
And only stale water for
What is an indecent thirst

Yes – we do believe there are
Perfect isles and quiet palms
Shady groves where rest
Might clothe us dry mariners

In this suspense of beauty
The garments of the king
Instinct with all life are
Intimate with dilemma

The seasons are his hands
And at night with his queen
He and she recreate
Knowledge and all fiction

Their love is like blood or
Wind or rain or shadow
Covering and impelling us
As we too cross the light

Birds are like the songs
This couple sing at dawn
When beside each other they
Compel every human joy

For we were heroes once
There was worship and rite
The beautiful was recharged
And made briefly viable

Yet strangers for all of time
Peripheral and marginal – we
Only walked about the walls
Never knew the inner city

Beneath a slim young moon
At dusk as sea swells crimson
No wave breaks to whiteness
Where we might simply pause -

Lightly rest from going and
Desist from working the ship
For suddenly human amity
Is excelled by our vision

For this is the truthful land
Island of clairvoyance
Animated by the person
Of the king and queen

The feminine is their principle
Through which they command
Just as lovers submit so
The king and queen inform

There is only one year
In this circle of avowal
Where each instant second
Witnesses their marriage

We know we too shall fall
Be buried alone at sea
Dropped astern into the water
Into void solitaire deep -

Regardless of suffering
Such was our strength in life
We never failed nor relented
For our love exceeded love

TWENTY TWO

In the pastures of the lion
We walked for all of time
And then as we diminished
We became cold and unaware

Sycamores and plane trees
Now lose their animal life
Running slower than the blood
The river darkens in its flow

Oblivious time is moving
As light turns and falls
Not one moment may we hold
Or simply apprehend

There are no mirrors here
Of colourless unearthly glass
As fish sink into the lake
And no hawks appear

We enter to a world of vision
Where all is only changeless
So much could have been
If we had only trusted

At night we briefly slept
Lying down on rough stone
About our heads stars hunted
For the lonely and indigent

Imperfection of this life
All its moral perjury
Like a dry mineral shoreline
Or outline of a broken arch —

Like a marble pyramid that
Has collapsed and lost its form
Each stone still retains
Part of beauty's vanished order

The feet of night approach
As days disperse like deer
All the sheaves have fallen
To the curving knife

This is the perfect 22threshold
Where faultless on the grass
Life becomes invisible
And we have no time

TWENTY THREE

THE hunger of animal life
Driving each human form
Like hawks or swallows who
Pursue what they do not know -

An impetus to raise walls
To mark the earth with paths
Making statues and songs that
Can never be destroyed

Or lightness of young children
The beauty of old terraces
Where oleander and chamomile
Enhance all that we see

This triumph of constant loss
Which owns no possession
Delivering passion and idea
Before our house is derelict

We never knew our riches
Nor how these powdery hills
And steep coasts discounted us
Disregarding our charisma

It is we who were the dust
Without intent or purpose
We only emulated and repeated
Truths which were unspeakable

In the eyes of an ideal ship
There is no single voyage
For distance and destination
Are our only just foresight

We consider this living curve
And yet there is no way
For we are always on anchor
Under a changeless wind -

Wreckage ruin detritus
The press of unbearable hours
Like stone wheels milling
Refining beautiful love

For death is not oblivion
It is life that is unaware
Death only returns us to
Absolution of the possible

We walked surplus years
Not caring where we stood
And then – when we arrived
There was nothing apparent

Lyrical and perfect walls
Genuinely grey and precise
Without life or recollection
As human experience wanders -

Toward an abandoned lighthouse
With its lenses and windvane
Yet there were no ships
Nor mariners awaiting our signal

This loneliness of terminus
Where if our aim was true
We shall have surpassed life
And every gift of genius

TWENTY FOUR

HERE at the summit of light
All the terms of life appear
Birth demise and marriages
Where trees never lose their leaves

Here swallows fly perpetually
As do the swan and geese
Wells and cisterns never dry
Lakes are only plentiful

Here young men and women
Give themselves without reprieve
For of the candid human body
Nothing can be said

No one turns in retrospect
To look upon the range of time
Nor is there ambition here
Driven to apprehend the future

In the summit of light a bird
Glides without endeavour
Unseen in the wind its song
Remains unheard on earth

The beautiful is always there
Causal in untimely light –
A sound of rain before dawn
Senseless fertile and beneficent

Then age is a carnal knife
That cuts and scars our bones
Serrating and incising
Reducing us to cruel lines

Where all our days become
Marks that record each love
Solitude and desperate effort
To exceed what is unknown

The beauty and the treasury
Of brief and perfect youth
Its adoration and assertion
When ardour is disclosed –

There is no morality in that
Only one single flawless truth
To give more than to receive
So that our aim is true

TWENTY FIVE

WHAT is it that makes us perfect
Changeless and out of time
For having touched this vision
There can be no possible rest

Made animate we are in this
Drawn out so we may give -
Neither miracle nor phantasy
Nor work of human artifice

In autumn intricate with gold
Volatile and so flammable
Where we recollect our youth
Hidden in the grain we keep –

Formed to give our lives away
Pursuing what we do not know
As birds migrate in darkness we
Are going far beyond ourselves

Now buried in the year we are
Covered with cold wet leaves
From plough to sickle we endure
To stand in love a few warm days

Estranged from all of life
We are unmade by this truth
Like a lover who is undressed
To join with superior lightness

Bees and dragonflies depart
To where they store their kind
The phantasies of summer
Are hidden by renewed coldness

Swallows and swans have gone
Hummingbird and acute heron
Geese like a compass needle
Indicate how time is passing

In every contour of the light
As darkness falls behind us and
Sunlight gleams upon the roads
We now stand apart from life

Boats are hauled onto the shore
Sails and rudders stowed on land
Ingenuity secures its pause
Scythes require no more sharpness

Darkness is within us now
We no longer anticipate
The future is conceived elsewhere
Experience becomes unlimited

Allure of human sentience
That resists and surrenders -
If light is all we know on earth
There is no need for promise

TWENTY SIX

Evening days when sunlight
Falls darkly on the grass
Among the stones we walk
As if life always continued

Yellow now becomes blue
And the slow river cools
As time becomes fugitive
Retreats from old romance

Deer and fawn leave the fields
Re-enter the unlit woods
To sleep on beds of dry fern
Reliving an unseen kind

No more do marriages concern
Young and youthful lovers
Grain is stored and dry
As hearths are renewed

What to say as we diminish
Covered by shadow and leaves
Without impression on the grass
It is as if we never slept

As if the truth of affection
Had never been exchanged
As in a light rain we walk
Only glad to be refreshed

For only moral kindness moves
Here in this broad world
Nothing else composes time
So that there is no death

Like a rare music that few hear
Or admire and keep within them
If we might love without object
We go beyond all person

So let us make this ceremony
Its rites of dispossession
Where we lightly sacrifice
Our passion to the rising sun

Then the universe will stand
Before us exposed and firm
And we justly shall become
The king and queen of beauty

TWENTY SEVEN

UNDERFOOT the yellow leaves
Are thin and lightly driven
By a warm south wind that
Misleads us with false season

We are mirrored by the sky
Yet hidden by a passing cloud
Our rituals and utmost pleasure
Might not eclipse that force

What alert lives exist
Beyond us and compelling
Animals and birds whose
Reason is our first influence

Patient and so ageless they
Pass about us in their course
Beautiful and revealing in
How they re-enact volition

Like the discerning panther
There for all of time
Even though you died you
Married us to diurnal life

Like the peripheral lions
Patrolling inaudibly
Whose sweetness and vision
Informed human thinking

Like the leopardess of love
Who joined us in the world
You were phenomenal and
Our passion was only yours

Like the hound with whom we walked
Who lay beside us on the grass
Your company was perfect
And your easy footstep

Like the super-aerial hawks
Observing and most reserved
Stalking and yet beneficent
Who affirmed every way

Like the initial heron whose
Flight began our song
You always went ahead and
We followed your just measure

Like the small bronze snake
Who for millennia gazed
Always warm upon the earth
Familiar to all kinship

Like the cats and their darkness
And their electricity
To all these pure creatures
Our gratitude is due

For our bodies are identical
Hearts breath and blood
Just as in touch and intimation
We imitate each other

Yet unlike us they do not
Forsake explicit honesty
Neither killing nor destroying
Without willing purpose

Both the single origin of death
And also its one terminus
They do not need our signs
Of ambivalent coercion

Nor do they ever covet
The sunlight or midnight
Wind and rainfall are their voice
And obedience to heaven

TWENTY EIGHT

IF the perfect work of art
Is soundless and unspeakable
Cannot be seen in light
Nor outlined by touch –

What season is it on earth
When lovers meet and sing
Of beauty and assurance
Of complete abundance

How is it we then cross
That weightless and transparent
Threshold and perceive
The numinous beyond time

Is there one just moment
During this earthly passage
When truth is unbreakable
And perfectly kind -

For you who wore dark colours
In the night and when
You undressed and summoned me
You became the universe

Ingenious were your hands
And your perfumed mouth
Filled me with the taste
Of all the stars at rest

The sweetness of your shape
Beside me during sleep
And your deep internal warmth
Which was all promise –

Walking with you in winter
When the woods were stripped
And the air sharp with cold
Your beauty was miraculous

Then to plough to sow to reap
To fell and cut the wood
To build the plough
To gather and to store the seed –

Before sowing and to forge
By fire the iron sickle to reap
To stand naked beneath midnight
To marry and together sleep

So we loved the animals and birds
Were honest in our lucid speech
Knew the words to re-enact
How all of life became entire

Creatures of silvery candescence
Walking beneath an awning
Of unbound lives – we were
Joined by the air we breathed

TWENTY NINE

HOMEWARD across frozen lakes
Descending lifeless black rivers
The evening sacrifice arrives
Its head inclined to submission

The silver rainfall hidden
In that unspeaking light
Is like the genius of a bell
Sounding throughout darkness

Skies stream with vain blood
The passion of a day declines
Coldness rests upon our skin
Where we forged the act of loving

Between the starry performance
And the gorgeous animal
Is this supernatural
Obscurity of a human heart

Or solitude and its precision
Enduring and indifferent
As a deer crossing a field
In the hour before sunrise

Just as we improvise
Our simple life and breathe
This paradise we then express
Is unaware of death

As now the universe puts on
A robe of perfect fashion
Its one superlative desire
Is stripped and given reason

Light of the year now dresses
In a soft grey filmy mask
Wandering the domain of night
Printless and without affection

Then far within the human body
An inner flame is cast
Changeless and perpetual
Indestructibly beyond life

Never to be extinguished
Nor in any way declined
It is a sea of treasure
Where love secures its heat

There honesty is like a guest
Akin to happiness
As we collect about the flames
In disregard of all time

That fire is our lively fate
Although we cannot reach it
Its impulse – like a vigil
Attends upon our weakest effort

Like worn apparel – we
Disguise within our kind
This luminous and visceral
Tissue of one just pursuit

So we become unnerved
Do not believe in truth
Struck by this perfect beauty
Of unspeakable experience

THIRTY

In the deadening of winter
Shadows among shadows go
A hawk gazing at its prey
A vague sun declining

The darkened river is still
As carbon or mineral
On the lake no breath moves
No deer come nervously to drink

A wing of geese in echelon
Circles the low dark sky
Above the evening fields where
Winter obscures the cold air

Like quiet foxes and coyotes
Who have patrolled this hill
For millennia wandering here
Fashioning hollows and giving birth

As night settles on the land
Darkness rises from the earth
We kindle fire into flame
The immediacy of warmth

So experience is reduced
As nil becomes our medium
When the bevelled edge of light
Cuts apart our simple story

These boreal days a bright king
Walks the land without pause
Where his woman sings of
The stations of all time

She holds a mirror to the world
Where coldness adheres and
Conceals how it is we love
How we struggle to recall

Sun and moon like men and women
Transform as they pursue
There is no solitude for
We are only animal in kind

Life rests upon a bed
Where the lovers once inspired
Days and nights to simply kiss
Like stars in the embrace of dawn

Despite our wounds and grievance
Nothing can resist that light
Even crocus and the swallows
Exceed our small duration

Regardless how we count the hours
There is only one telling
How human life receives its passion
Then forgets until revived

Now lying on the grass among
The stones like a cloud going
We shall become the sea and
That which makes the waves run

We shall be the wind as
It wanders among empty trees
The body of the seasons and
Celibate and promising air

We shall become the birds who
Know how to travel and
In time and frequence circulate
As if they were a worldly blood

Then there is the earth that
Never moves and only changes
Stone dust of sand fields
And weight of all our ways

THIRTY ONE

AN oak tree with the moon
In its dark hair as carmine
Reflects upon the river's ice
With tangerine and magenta bars

A hawk flees the night
As we abjure another year
Lightless is our hemisphere
With the grey depth of an ocean

If a man and woman were to walk
Among the diamonds of affection
The way of human amity
As it moves about the earth –

Then the light within their vision
Would be apart from time
There would be no body
And no singular admission

Arrows would never fly
Nor missiles destroy cities
Rain would always bring to fields
Water from the ancient sky

In that song there is no death
No grief nor any misery
Only the direction of the weather
And the littleness of life

For when a man and woman join
The world is indestructible
They live beyond experience
And its animal kind

As they walk and breathe
And words move between them
The universe withdraws admiring
The beautiful at rest

So now as the year advances
Both superhuman and concentric
Time nooses us in its suspense
We apprehend its genius

This is no place for sorrow
Futility of recrimination
For each minute bears a cargo
Of compassion and design

THIRTY TWO

RAIN falls upon the hills
Our paths are printed on the grass
Among the stones above the river
For years we walked alone

Beneath the clouds we slept
As new leaves came and went
Small apples appeared and fell
Upon the earth and decayed

Light upon that yellow grass
Light falling on your hair
The universe does not know
The light we offer as devotion

You were a swan within
My heart and running lightly
Moving imperceptibly
Your blood was like the sun

Buried deep within my eyes
You were that clear white bird
You were the careless lioness
Whose ardour was all passion

Beauty of your perfect feature
Absolution of your figure
Your eyes whose radiance
Exceeds all life on earth

Then one day we awoke
Discovered that our lives had gone
Had flown away – departed
So we were free to love

To take the truly beautiful
By the hand and walk apart
Go where we were unseen
Giving ourselves to each other

Then effortless – our lives
Became only compassionate
As we wandered the universal
Coast hills groves and tracks

Then it was our work
To change those enduring
Who were oblivious – unaware
That kindness makes everything

Rain vanished with the morning
The grey river became blue
Reflecting back a candid sky
As heron geese and swans settled

Buried beneath the shallow hill
So many lives were interred
So much love and such grief
Now only given to the air

As light issues from a glass
And breaks into its elements
Inconspicuous and spectral
So we are dispersed in kind

I always hear you being called
By words I never say
Living speech is not enough
To tell of your complete absence

THIRTY THREE

THIS is our last voyage now
For we are far away at sea
Becoming all that we have ever
Spoken or done in time

We offered all our nakedness
To the world and its kind
Stripped of love and wealth
We crossed the unbound waves

Free of every threshold
Even bare of life itself
Dawn shows her perfect beauty
Damp and saline and exposed

There is no sound of engines
No motion of the decks
No isles nor ports where lovers
Simplify our old pain

All the languages and rites
Of people and their stories
Marriages and burials and
How children are exchanged -

We held those coins in our hand
And weighed all their years
Yet even metal has no voice
Compared to wind in our sail

The rotten timbers creak
As canvas tears and frays
Bronze is green and lines unwind
Our instruments become frail

There is a gate through which
We pass - of light and radiance
And having touched that shore
There is nowhere else on earth

Who knows what destination
Is prepared for our rest
Nothing is permanent and yet
Every move has consequence

Dolphin whale and grey seal
The callous sea itself
Slow white birds glide astern
Telling us nothing any more

Then as if crowned with horns
We are possessed and lively
Measured by a perfect music
We are joined in silent dance

If there is no body
And nothing can be said
This stillness and equilibrium
Becomes the voyage itself

THIRTY FOUR

SHIPS are sailing toward the city
Anchoring off the coast at night
Awaiting the touch of morning
To separate turbulent darkness

Millennia of vessels standing
With passages of every compass
So many ancient cargoes
Exchanged in easy avarice

This city spawned of commerce
Of worn brown coins and freight
Its lust and grain of humanity
Transformed into moral wealth

Squalls come and drag anchors
Tearing apart unbound canvas
Mariners grow old ashore yet
In their hearts they are on deck

No one dies at sea and
No children are born on ships
The boundless world of navigation
Is ageless and perpetual

Women of every conviction know
Those low cabins and narrow berths
A knowledge of what is forbidden
Once they step on land again

Where are the companions with whom
We sailed and walked those coasts
With oars of pinewood we carried
Timber of masts and folded sails

We slept at night upon the sand
Or in the shadow of groves
In closed rooms excluding the sun
We made love during afternoons

Now we walk this stony port
Under the trees to that harbour
To bend our necks in submission
At the world's translucent beauty

Where all that we know desists
The perfection of certain songs
Even the love we had shared
Now falls away from experience

Rinsed in fire – discreetly radiant
Submerged and subdued by suffering
Only we admit true promise
Among the streets of impostors

All that remains is a table
In a small bay on that island
Where in an avenue of cedars
We offered a lamp of understanding

Now this becomes our freedom
As we perceive all emptiness
And the pity of those dying
Who might apprehend no future

Alone beneath the palm trees
There remains one companion
Whose happiness is oblivious
And given - regardless of death

THIRTY FIVE

BALANCED within our lives
Is all gravity and time
And in our small circulation
Earth turns and returns

Islands with their young palms
Pine trees in the harbour
Cedars rooted in grey rocks
Where children hide and play

Those whom we kissed are gone
Those we loved do not appear
Their ships departed before light
As if they never knew our beds

Wearing rings and green tattoos
Marrying in those silvery hours
Those mariners never realised
That love was our subtle blade

We cut the simple fire within
Their golden bodies where they lay
Beside us in our white rooms -
Not one word was exchanged

The payment was in sorrow
The easy grief they changed
Pity and not the amorous
Was the pattern they unclothed

All night the wind was crying
The sea was broken into ice
Darkness disdained morning
Dawn stayed behind old stars

You took away our sleep then
So we became more vulnerable
We became deprived and
No one could be true

We lost our voices in those nights
Until we learned to sing
Could lament that just happiness
Of always being touched

The ships were never seen again
We soon forgot the arts of love
Sons became young men like trees
Who sailed aways in search of brides

So build yourself a ship of love
That will take you beyond
All that you might ever know
Or might one day recall

In that voyage of all time
Remember those who gave
So much life into your hands
Into your eyes and voice

THIRTY SIX

WHEN life is beaten thin like foil
Shining most perfectly
Reflecting days and sunlight
As if nothing had occurred

That gorgeous novel emptiness
Which reappears each morning
Refreshing us with its taste
Going further than we know -

A superhuman force so
Immortal and unearthly
Which drives men and women
Toward each other in their eyes

Made of motive shadow they
Are like a tide within the sea
Unaware they are compelled
Throughout their admiration

There is a ship called happiness
Whose clear genius of ways
Can always take a passenger
Who pays with one just life

Few lovers speak of those isles
Nameless coast of redolence
Where white birds only sing
A true confusion of desire

We walk a thousand years
Yet there is no destination
As you and I look upon
The beauty of all solitude

The origin of human grief
Like a fine coin that none possess
Passes silently between hands
As we pursue affection -

In the promises we give in life
Our only freedom lies
Both magnetic and yet fatal
Loss makes us more than light

So they draw the curtains as
They embark at night upon
That beloved ship where sleep
Joins the lovers in all ways

THIRTY SEVEN

WE are all faithlesss now
Sometimes pausing to touch
Wreaths of grief or affection
With passages of casual love

This little white boat sailing
The ultra and aquamarine
You really were a turquoise bird
Ephemeral with all of time

Beauty of your hull and sails
Perfection of your wake astern
You were a ship of stone yet
One wounded day you took us

For you we now weep
Not for sorrow nor despair
But for joy of wealth received
For you conveyed everything

You took our hearts – little boat
Left us on a mineral island
Where – as queen among pines
Your final gift was prolific

The morality of death here
Is our work on earth
As we embrace not what
We leave but go towards

In marriage for a brief while
Men and women become
King and queen who celebrate
The clarity of imperative

On that ritual floor they
Are performing and mimetic
They re-enact the universe
Both visual and acoustic -

The infidelity of death where
Death does not discard us
When we become invisible
And none observe us any more

How might we justify our words
The many footsteps on this earth
So as to walk beyond
What we might never say -

To give more than we receive
To recognise that bearing
When stripped of speech we
Have nothing to retract

How many lives must we endure
How many loves relinquish
How many years of effort
Before we are free of kind

Old captain pilot mariner friend
Let us cast off our last minutes
Journey beyond our eyes where
There is no darkness visible

There is no love equal to this
For we have lost everything
In the city of light there is
No body and in that city – no one

THIRTY EIGHT

NOW as time runs away
And we become defined
Where are the beautiful companions
With whom we once walked

Where are the lovers and friends
With whom we shared bare rooms
Or danced with when there was
No music on the island

Where are the dry sandy paths
That led between the pines
To the closed bays where we loved
And fell asleep in our nakedness

The ships have come and gone
White vessels on the ultramarine
As we stood on the deck watching
Our wake vanish into the light

No one knew we were going
Away from each other then
That death had already marked
The day of our return

It was death who had clipped
Our tickets as we embarked
We – who thought that happiness
Could have no destination

Yet for a sudden transient moment
Human amity and kindness
Found an earthly dwelling
Revealing its brief permanence

In summer when the sky was perfect
And life reformed a clear zenith
We turned away from that distance
Where the sun kept its ancestors

THIRTY NINE

A PITILESS and neglectful sky
Steady sound of mute snowfall
Roads disappear and recede
Sunless morning is without shadow

Snow now occludes the world
So many qualities of grey
As water paths and air – all one
Appear without artifice

There are no prints of any creature
No small bird skims the light
The beauty of the lifeless earth
Lies in this perfect stillness

On the river swans vanish
Asleep on a winter stream
Waking in a cloth of ice
As the current is subdued

What is this play of destiny
In this scene of bird and river
Of immutably perfect snowfall -
Reducing all consequence

Who knows what to say
When every sign is removed
Except for that naked torso
Whose warm hand touches us

A tint of carmine in the east
The living sweetness of your lips
That one just kiss which revives
All promise of our kind

The clear topaz in your eye
Catches us so firmly now
One vital and terrific glance
Moves us on our way for ever -

Soft blood running in a vein
Breath passing through our mouths
Love that drives us onward
Toward what is unspeakable

Yet even love cannot say
What impels us now
A quick sensation that creates
More than we might ever know

The snow falls as the sky
Undresses and allows her garment
To spill onto a somnolent world
So we are clothed in darkness

As the days race past us like
Arrows of clear bevelled light
We lose ourselves in boundless haste
Unaware of what occurred

For just as the snow obscures
All grass and paths on earth
So in days we misplace
Experience and its recollection

How in our lives do we transform
From child to youth to partner -
That perfect admiration in
The volition of a sanguine lover

This superhuman pursuit where
We locate the changeless creature
In this universe of recession
As the beautiful exceeds us

Those hammers which first formed
Us long ago - before speech
Was printed on our tongues
Before we knew of mastery

That destiny now takes us from
This world of winter and deceit
Of water light impersonal summit
Which is where our days await

That force of passion or of intellect
Which draws us from ourselves
How does that impulse cause
Swans to waken from their coldness

FORTY

WHO has the courage to be always
Alone to walk through darkness
Without a hand to touch
Or any words to change

Who speaks for years without
Being heard and who listens
More than says – offering
Easy speech to the vain

Refugees and migrants who
Have no place to rest
Their awareness is unfound
Within their hearts and eyes -

When there is only hunger
And no aqua-blue of days
Where coldness and solitude
Are the companions of time

The only friends they have
Are the voices they hear
Visions clearly promising
Taking them away from kind –

When there are no songs
Only recollections in the air
That exist without purpose
Of motive or ambition

Courage is their liaison
Imperative as the spring
When colours rise from earth
Renewing the force of life -

The caress of wind and rain
Upon the simple hours
Quietness of those lost hills
When there is nothing moving

Lightness is their midnight
That only they perceive
Apparent beyond the world
Charging all their love

Such terrific moral force
Impels their election as
They are obliged to pursue
An unbearable truth

Only complete defeat or
The compulsion of solitude
Might approach this beauty
Exceeding grief and thirst

For even when accomplished
As they resign from life
Their inner sight of landscape
Makes compassion their home

FORTY ONE

Just as a ship whose timber
Has been replaced year by year
Nothing remains of that first vessel
Yet the ship continues to sail

So too in life renewed
We are remade and refound
Yet nothing exists of that first
Person who once walked on earth

There is the green of spring
And then the green of summer
Nothing changes and the cause
Of all movement is our eyes

In this circulating world
Of so much experience where
Only when we love do we
Recall that first design -

That original form where lovers
Recreate their new life
Reviving this round world
Upon a boundless rim

Here is moral endurance
Greatness of all solitude
Here is the flame and sea-wave
Lake river cistern and well

Here the genius of true life
Beauty perfectly clear -
We stand as if in a gateway
And through its arms we pass

Here is our sunlight and
Here our miraculous night
Look – those are the creatures
Small lives always attending

They know of our fragility
Of all likely decease
Their privacy is unspoken
As we pretend to know life

Yet foxes and coyotes patrolled
These low hills for millennia
Long before any human print
Walked upon these slopes -

Vineyards orchards meadows
Paths made by deer where
A forest discloses no motion
And there are no messengers

Here is a passing word
Full of cold and darkness
And there is transformation
Which no one ever discerns

Nothing remains of our first idea
Vessel which none recall
Yet the love that we reform
Tempers every possible change

This is the apparent man
Woman without remorse
Who gambles away her vision
Knowing her aim to be true

FORTY TWO

WE crossed the line today
Running beyond horizon
Now none might observe
The nature of our journey

Our vessel goes as if
Without wind in the sails
As if the ship itself knew
Its own courage and impulse

There are many wives here
And so many husbands
Going in and out of the light
As if the decks were nuptial

To have lost greatly is
To have given without lease
And so we gain the world
That we are about to leave

In this roar of solitude
Emptiness of driven rain
Beauty leaves us nothing
But stones upon the sand

We perceive ourselves now
As in an ideal circle
Seeking one just resemblance
That we might admire

This single lightless second
Falls perfectly between
The unseen and the true
Where the universe resides -

A spherical perfection
Of knowing we stand apart
With gratitude for the love
That made us first

Like a perfect ship of kind
Launched by the grief of losing
Made of gestures of affection
Beautiful in its circling -

A masterpiece we prepare
To take us out of life
That has no place in time
Is not impelled by any loving

Neither spring nor winter
Nor summer's candid vision -
This complete work possesses
No earthly human bearing

So we foresee our lives
And reach for our destiny
That we impersonate
Becoming strangely free

Like a white bird of passage
Barely exposed at night
Or like the deer in a dream
When there are no witnesses -

Not even elemental – we
Can hold nothing in our arms
For all that we embrace
Is soon resolved to air

Not even virtue might compel
This flawless presence
Whose genius is flagrant
As if supremely amorous

For nothing can be told
Not given nor forgiven
Just seen and dismissed as
An unspeakable act of love

FORTY THREE

This voyage owns no duration
No pace nor destination
It is a journey in the eyes
And in the speech of birds

Sails make no earthly sound
And the flat sea as it moves
Along the whitened hull is silent
No voice commands the decks

Navigation is unknown
We are dominated by the heaven
Conjugated by the planets
Without a single response

There is no death on board
No birth nor any romance
Marriage and adultery do not
Exist nor is there deceit -

A universal man and woman
One kind of living only
Familiar with suffering and grief
So necessary to conceive joy

Rocks islands dawn twilight
Odour of sweet saline air
The discipline of loneliness
Makes each day possible -

Captivated by all illusion
Ambition passion and remorse
Where sleep falls upon the vessel
Like a damp irresistible net

There is only one passage
Which no one can tell
And even in the retrospect
Solitude remains captain

Promise is our only compass
Wind the kindness of light
Timbers of the ship are
Made of leaves and of grass

Soon the heart deceases
And soon breath is paused
The currency of blood stilled
Yet the passage is changeless

Travelling further than genius
More excellent than truth
Our course is unbearable
This perfection of the universe -

Like a charioteer who circles
Knowing only of one track
Whose burning axle and wheel
Cannot survive victory

What to say of the voyage
If there is only one bearing
If humility is superhuman
In this unworldly endeavour -

In this mystery of duality
How we are dispossessed
Causing us to rest our oars
To walk ashore at last -

That sky where animals patrol
Migrating through time as if
Those pastures and grasslands
Were always indestructible

At last we look upon the stones
That signed our ancient course
Shadows and impression where
We once loved and slept

FORTY FOUR

THERE is a ship of genius
Crossing the crimson seas
Where perfect mariners sing
Of women they once loved

They have forgotten the cities
The coinage of those towns
As across the reticent seasons
They let the vessel make a way

No one dies aboard the ship
Birds live among the sails
Sometimes a lion and leopardess
Walk the decks in solitaire night

There is an isle called *Romance*
Where the vessel comes about
Setting its anchors in the sand
As the crew lightly swim ashore

There beneath the palm trees
And avenues of pure cedar
Women take these men and
Strip them of all remorse

The mariners rest ashore
Among the rocks and fields
As women make beds of promise
And soon the boat disappears

Just as the captain only wants
A wife to be at his side
In the glossy nights when sleep
Covers the sky with dry stars –

So the young navigator
With a sheaf of charts and compass
Is the only one who knows
The course to this flawless isle

On the wooden ship of genius
Just like a bride and groom
Kindness and fidelity are
Quietly and ritually joined

The universe allows this gift
Like a bird dives to water
With beauty overwhelming
The moral experience of grief

Beware as you enter that ship
To know what you believe
For without oars or pilot even
Winged canvas the vessel goes

If your aim is not true
You should not walk that deck
For the bubble in the compass
Was not formed by life on earth

Patient faithful and so strong
You might one day reach
Those entire isles of love
If you know those songs

There the women will take
All your sorrow and fatigue
And bathed by their kindness
Your blood will be renewed

A sound of bees and cicadas
Will assuage your thirst
When you sleep the women
Shall quietly remove your heart

Be aware as you set sail
That you shall not return
To the orchards and the gardens
For you are now alone at sea

Each word that you speak
Like a footstep advances
The vessel across green water
Where white birds are silent

Remember this election
And its complete ideal
For no one knows your freedom
Having gone beyond the world

Then perfectly they appear
Those who have apprehended
Truth and abandoned all
Expectation of affection

What is it they know
That so exceeds our lives
Going beyond all experience
Even the gifts of love

FORTY FIVE

HOW to say what we do not know
Or to depict only our vision
If all of life is a vehicle
Happiness must always go further

Now the light transforms itself
Less fierce and less transparent
Its grain has been harvested
And the sky begins to sleep

Seeds are prepared for rest
For their long interment
And lovers – satisfied by days
Begin to close their eyes

The only one who now succeeds
Is the solitary and quiet
Whose passion has gone beyond
Exceeding love on earth

Cadence is a great gift
This is what light brings
All lovers know this truth
As they revisit memories

In the mansions of our heart
The world has now retired
For the joy of disillusion is
The finest of all pleasures

So light becomes thin and bare
More lucid and weightless
As our bodies justly assume
That time has been perfected

What were those coins we handled
And how did we exchange our kind
Those who pursue only happiness
Cannot apprehend life

For virtue moves us toward
The future where we become
All that we never were
On earth in our endeavour

Some exceed human love
Because they were simply able
To give more than they received
From days and existence

FORTY SIX

A SOVEREIGN lies upon the grass
Its body made of light and dust
Of warmth fused with breath
Where unseen blood is flowing

This is our heart and speech
Water that conveys us
Filling eyes with vision and
Fluid of every passion

Blood owns three songs on earth
Of promise kin and amity
Of these avowal is the greatest
That human life might share

To pledge is our one freedom
Contrary to the adulterous
As friendship makes for kind
So renewing us in time

Blood mixed with honey
With water from the ground
Is offered in both love and grief
At a point where we touch -

Where hand in hand we go
With no shadow nor impression
No print upon the grass
Leading where none can say

For blood dries without stain
There is no trace of life
On broken stones or walls
Where quadrupeds step at night

Then when the fallen drops
Blacken old dry paths
Every bird knows that death
Is our only possible sign -

Blood of midwinter dusk
Where the sky runs carmine
Scarlet autumnal hills
Where trees dress in crimson -

Blood of vernal poppies
When the deceased lie beneath
The voice of singing birds
Blood of lions in summer

This blood is like a king who
Rules our world with impetus
Causing lovers to be sovereign
Compelling with desire

All that remains is for ghosts
To crave one drink of life
Blood upon thin grey lips
To revive all that is passed

FORTY SEVEN

WHEN we were young kings
We played in the light
Now we accomplish
Such pleasure in our mind

Then we knew the heroes
And the songs they performed
Familiar with all they achieved
With their unbreakable spears

We knew the arrows and
All the fine blades that shaped
How it was their sonority
Informed how we lived -

Chains racing on their wheels
Cries of animals at night
Hunting or pairing as
They procreated wonderfully

There was one spear called patience
Whose iridescent passion
Was like music as it flew
Craving for affection

That spear moved in harmony
Disciplined and precise
Unseen – striking perfectly
So life might be renewed

The spear turned on air
Splitting apart all fruit
Cutting open the wind
So drops of blood appeared

Few apprehend this missile
Of life that darts in flight
Like a viper's needle-tongue
Of unbearable solitude

Like sails on a boat or
Sharp wings of a passage bird
Shadows that move in water
Or sparks rising to the night –

There is no name for this
Ardent force of time
Where shadows circulate and
Noose us in their days

Only in the stillness when
We simply close our eyes
Does the spear secure a target
Breaking the human heart

In that death we are remade
Offered a brief new purpose
As the solitary is felled
Without any solemn words

Lying on the earth at last
Our head upon a stone
The aerial world above us
Home of hawks and falcons -

So we are unnerved
As this javelin of unseen light
Is fired and takes us away
To where there is no time

When we were those kings
Our aim was always true
We pursued the great world
Found and made our love

In each life there is a moment
When justice becomes beautiful
Then the leaves begin to fall
As age takes away our kind

Even the stones we raised
Were broken by the wind
Our monuments became sand
Our names dried into ash

Yet a force that is hidden
In the truths we defined
Shall never be destroyed for
Then we were just kings

FORTY EIGHT

THE golden tissue that you draw
About your shoulders now
Perpetual indestructible
That no hand might remove -

Such luminous rites of life
Anointment with charisma
Like the blade in your grasp
Both subtle and invisible

May this be your springtime
As you alone ascend
With a promise that now seals
All your destined footsteps

May a million silent doves
Descend from the air as
A thousand years surround
You with their admiration

May all the beneficial ghosts
Hover close about your ways
Guiding you with their vision
And suspense of perfect song

May lakes trees hills and stones
Only flourish in your sight
One common wealth of earth
This isle - its birds and clouds

You become the trusted
Force that acts like time
Joining lives in one union
So exceeding private kind -

An agency of truth that binds
With words that you profound
Both principal and mirror that
Illuminates these islands

The future and its past now meet
Upon the ground you deliver
For no one might diminish
These instruments you present

So this beauty you inhabit
Received transformed and worn
Shall always be our just vessel
Crowned with complete honour

Out of earth comes treasury
Oil of purest light
Almost fluid in its kind
Both timeless and impermanent

Touched upon the forehead you
Become unworldly now
Undisclosed in slow dawn
Cadmium crimson and of chrome

Free of all speech and saying
Surrounded by the gorgeous sea
At last uncreated you
Become all that you were

Those buried giants sleeping
Convey you in their arms
Their hands move beneath the fields
Taking you toward new rivers

You honour tombs of long ago
Imploring their perfection
Where there is only darkness
You now receive such radiance

Upon a threshold where all action
Is ineffective and so weightless
Crowned with beauty you advance
To change your body for a garland

FORTY NINE

I AM the voice of the unseen
Yet you shall never know me
Listen - as my words disperse
What I say refers to nothing

All the patience of the world
Like water goes to water
We cannot moderate our time
As we pause on the edge of life

Lightly in love we are formed
To appear and then vanish
Then in years we run away
From all the gifts received

All the days of life expire
Each one polishing your soul
As the last morning appears
Then you might see my face

There I stand always waiting
As your promise glimpses me
Or perhaps in love you saw
My perfect form more closely

Pursuing all possible ways
Complete in our division
We shall become so true
Just you and I together

As a quiet deer approaches
A hunter who only waits
Or a falcon cuts open the wind
Taking an oblivious hare -

We must slow our quickness
Become so still none observe
Our passing or our company
As we stand about to withdraw

As a woman gives herself
To a man whom she elects
Or a man offers his vision to
A woman if she walks with him -

Now we await this coming
Proof of all we have dared
Convinced yet still desperate
As a groom before a bride

That became the only voyage
More furtive than wave or shadow
For even beyond sleep we move
Conveyed by just admiration -

Glittering benign transparent
Empty and fully spacious
Without death or any ruin
I am more than you conceived

A gracious sun in hiding
Where love is undivided
We are lacking in distinction
One duration just the same

By the faith of my body
And the innumerable days
If we think about each other
We shall always be moved

FIFTY

THERE is a panther in the night
That only we perceive
By the odour of its breath
Who charges all our loving

Unbearable truth of this
Perfect animal torso
The lightness of her eyes is
Apparent beyond the world

Such terrific moral impetus
Impels our election and
We are obliged to pursue
That untouchable vitality

In our darkness there is
No motion of that candid fire
No body for the panther
Is without one just desire

Only complete defeat or
The compulsion of solitude
Might approach this beauty
Exceeding grief and thirst

Even when accomplished
As we resign from life
The sight of this creature
Is our gesture of compassion -

A soft and gentle scarlet
Where she assumes her place
Surrounded by an infinite
Completely perfect darkness

Before her we are stripped
Cease to breathe and know
And as she overwhelms us
All human joy is released

There can be no song of this
No kiss nor slow touch
As we slowly move apart
And enter to her universe

How yesterday and tomorrow
Simply do not exist
Like white dust on a summer road
Or the intrinsic calm of winter

Neither honesty nor surrender
Might reform this oblivion
We cannot calculate the truth
Where we give ourselves away

So much inventiveness of love
Only leading to this place
Where numerous vermilion stars
Rain lightly upon the earth

The mystery and the beauty
Of a river and an upland lake
The grey internal life of
Cold water moving or at rest -

Naked of any quality
We walk those arid shores alone
Admitting the unspeakable
Born of a woman's blood

AFTERWORD

WHAT is sovereign in this poetry is the vision that is compressed and compounded by the presence and complete agency of metaphor in this world: metaphor being our only source of action and its superlative condition of love being our one act of potential freedom in life. It is our awareness of death which drives this appeal and impetus of metaphor, for there we do not repeat or imitate but we move away from what we know and have received and travel towards a new and impersonal universe of nature. Nature is paradoxically both our origin and our end and our vision then becomes the medium that enables us to desist from such just compulsion, allowing us to withdraw gently. A metaphor is a mask that covers one identity and conveys another *persona*, conveying meaning from one to another; hence two different masks can transmit the same message even though they are unlike. So what is that initiating and hypothetical impulse which leads us to consider and to think of something else in a manner which we were not previously aware? Even the first personal pronoun is in itself a metaphorical origin of sorts, establishing a medium which allows us to apprehend and then to judge, in the same way that a syllogism operates. The word 'I' has no personal substance nor property and is simply an envelope which bears consciousness within its empty vessel. Metaphor is thence a *vehicle*, one which delivers meaning that was previously unavailable and it is this reception of significance which moves us through time. Compulsion is *not* a source of metaphor in this original or unique sense, for compulsion simply recapitulates a past occurrence or event. True metaphor generates new signification and so transmits the bearer onward in time whereas any gesture or message that is compelling simply repeats past experience and does not innovate nor create new proficiency. It is this impulse which drives an individual through their life to the final point of decease, death being a quality or situation which both causes and evades all possible metaphor, always circling our way.

Kevin MᴄGʀᴀᴛʜ was born in southern China in 1951 and was educated in England and Scotland; he has lived and worked in France, Greece, and India. He was an associate of the Department of South Asian Studies and poet laureate at Lowell House, Harvard University. Publications include, *Fame* (1995), *Lioness* (1998), *Maleas* (2002), *The Sanskrit Hero* (2004), *Flyer* (2005), *Comedia* (2008), *Stri* (2009), *Jaya* (2011), *Supernature* (2012), *Heroic Krsna* and *Eroica* (2013), *In The Kacch* and *Windward* (2015), *Arjuna Pandava* and *Eros* (2016), *Raja Yudhisthira* (2017), *Bhisma Devavrata* (2018), *Vyasa Redux* (2019), *Song Of The Republic* (2020), *Fame* (2023), *On Friendship* (2024), *Romance – The Only Life* (2024), *Causality In Homeric Song* (*forthcoming* 2025) and *Dionysos: Nature Without Instinct* (*forthcoming* 2025). McGrath lived in Cambridge, Massachusetts, with his family.

Type Settings & Fonts:
PERPETUA TILTING MT
GARAMOND — Garamond

www.ingramcontent.com/pod-product-compliance
Lightning Source LLC
Chambersburg PA
CBHW081339120626
46546CB00011B/3411